ADVANCED TECHNIQUES FOR
Plug-Cut Herring

AF207251

by **Phil Pirone**
President, Pro-Cure Bait Scents

**Frank Amato
Publications**

All inquiries should be addressed to:
Frank Amato Publications, Inc.
P.O. Box 82112 • Portland, Oregon 97282
www.amatobooks.com • (503) 653-8108

All subject/scenic photos by Phil Pirone unless otherwise noted
Cover and book design by Tony Amato

SB ISBN-13: 978-1-57188-493-0   SB UPC: 0-81127-00339-6

Printed in China

Contents

Author Phil Pirone admires another beautiful Chinook salmon that fell prey to a plug-cut herring. On some days all these big salmon want is meat. A properly rolling herring, injected with scent, can often get you hooked up!

Introduction

In the August/September 1992 issue of *STS* magazine I co-authored the feature article "Successful Plug-Cut Herring Techniques" with guide Gary 'Gilly' Gilchrist. At that time I was just the observer/writer. It was Gilly who shared his wealth of knowledge on plug-cut fishing, and not me. But it was when I fell in love with catching chrome-bright salmon on plug-cut bait. It just pressed all of my buttons, and it really turned me on. It's hard to believe that collaboration was almost 20 years ago, and during those 20 years I've had the opportunity to fish with some of the best plug-cut fishermen on the West Coast. And more importantly, to learn

ADVANCED TECHNIQUES FOR PLUG-CUT HERRING

from them. So I'm thinking, after 20 years since the first article, it just might be time to update the original masterpiece. Ironically, I have just finished a brand-new Pro-Cure DVD called *"Secrets of the Pros - Successful Plug Cutting Techniques."* In many ways it parallels this book. The DVD is extremely comprehensive and runs almost 2 hours long. So whether you read this book, or watch the DVD, you will come away with something of value. If you are a novice it will get you out there competently fishing herring. If you are an advanced plug-cut angler there are tips in here for you too. So let's get started.

SELECTING HERRING

Short of jigging up your own herring we have three choices in buying herring. Seasonally you can buy freshly bagged herring on ice in areas like the early fall Buoy 10 fishery. But most of us are buying frozen herring either trayed and bagged by size, or frozen and vacuum packed. As owner of Pro-Cure I get to fish with a lot of top guides and I can tell you very few of them fish fresh-bagged herring on ice. They haven't been starved, so they are usually soft baits, and hard to keep on the hooks, especially in heavy river or tidal currents. And the scales are so delicate that by the time you have a bait plug-cut and rigged there are more scales on your hands than the fish. This situation can be remedied slightly by opening the bag of fresh herring and sprinkling in a very healthy shot of dry Pro-Cure Brine 'N Bite powder. Then add a fistful of non-iodized salt, seal the bag and place it back on ice. If you give your bait an hour or longer in the dry powder and salt it will significantly improve the fishability of fresh bait.

Most of us will fish frozen herring. It comes in 6 basic sizes, and these vary by processor and seasonal harvest. Basically the smallest sizes are color coded by label or print on the package. Orange and Red are the smallest, and may be fished whole, as they are usually too small to plug-cut. The next size up is Green label, and these baits are perfect for ocean Coho and Chinook, and river salmon too. In fact, probably the two most popular sizes for plug-cutting are Greens, and one size larger Blue label. I hesitate to give sizes, as the sizes vary by processor and size availability. Many times I'll hear guides say they are fishing big Greens or small Blues, meaning the Blues that were packaged could almost be big Greens. Or big Greens could almost be small Blues. The next larger size is Purples, and the largest are Black label. For many years anglers had to have Purple or Black label herring to fish the river mouths for the bigger fall Chinook, but quite honestly I rarely see anything larger than a Blue label fished anymore. I think part of that is the returning fall Chinook are smaller in size, and the 50- and 60-pounders of yesteryear are rarely seen today. Also the larger-size herring are hard to find, and much more costly to fish. The average tray for frozen herring costs between $4.50 and $7.00 a tray, and with Purple and Black label herring you get 5 to 6 on a tray. With Purples you'll get 6 to 8. With Blues and Greens you'll usually get 10 to 12 baits per tray, so if you can get bit on the smaller sizes why waste the money?

Having the most freshly harvested and processed herring can be critical in a tough bite. I will regularly have guides call me and say "ABC processor just got in a bunch of Green label herring that were caught three weeks ago. Do you want a case?" Now if this phone call comes in late January, and you plan on starting your plug-cut herring fishing on the Columbia in mid March for springers, you'd better jump on some bait. However, if you are not sure

Top, a Green label herring; Middle, a Blue label; and Bottom, a Purple label herring. The Black label is even larger than a Purple. These are the four most common sizes for plug-cutting bait.

of when the bait was harvested, or how long it will take you to go through it, always go with the vacuum-packed frozen bait over the bagged frozen bait. Just like when you vacuum pack beef or chicken, the food in the vacuum pack stays fresher much longer than bagged or paper-wrapped food, and so does bait. If you plug-cut a vacuum-packed herring processed 6 months ago it will cut bloody red, and smell fresh caught. That same bait bagged will smell stale, and the internal organs and blood will look more like coffee milk than bloody red. If you are in a wide-open ocean Coho bite you may get bit, but fishing the bubble at our ocean inlets, or upriver, where the fish are picky biters, tired old bait is far from ideal. So when you have the chance always go with trayed vacuum-packed bait over the bagged, unless you personally know when the bagged bait was harvested. Again, if you are going to consume freshly harvested bait right away it can be trayed and bagged and frozen with no problem. If you know when the bait was harvested and you plan on fishing it right away, frozen trayed in bags will work just fine. Under any other conditions go with the trayed vacuum-packed bait for freshness.

Always buy starved herring. When herring are netted they are usually feeding. Their bellies are full of food, and they are soft. The best herring is starved before processing. The bait is put in floating ocean cages in areas

Tired old bait (top) versus freshly harvested vacuum-packed tray bait. You can get by with tired old bait for ocean Coho on many days, but for a bubble fishery, or up-river fishery, where Chinook are picky biters, using old bait puts you at an extreme disadvantage. It your herring don't cut blood red you shouldn't be fishing them.

where plankton and other floating food is not available to the penned bait. The bait is forced to live off of its stored fat, and its belly tightens, and so do the scales. After starving their baits the best processors hand brail the baits into 5-gallon pails, and then the bait is instantly electrocuted. The more gently the bait is handled, the more scales stay on the bait. This is critical in selecting bait because when the bait is plug-cut and it rolls, it flashes from the sunlight's reflection on the bait's scales. If most of the scales are knocked off due to poor processing there will be no flash as the herring rolls. More flash means more visibility from further distances for predator fish like salmon. So when selecting trayed bait look for those baits with the least scales missing. Also make sure you look for herring that have slender, flat bellies, not round and cigar shaped. Many folks will tell you when selecting frozen herring look for black eyes, but I have seen the freshest baits with white dots on their eyes after they have been frozen. Look for baits that have snowy white bellies, and avoid baits with yellow bellies, yellow or tannish fins and tails. Avoid baits with dried-out, shredded fins and tails. Any yellowing or discoloration means older bait. However if there is a shortage of freshly processed herring, or no herring at all, sometimes we are forced to fish old bait, or bait missing scales. If that is the case we'll cover how to make that tired old bait fish as well as possible in just a bit.

BRINING AND DYING HERRING

In 1992 Pro-Cure introduced its Brine 'N Bite Bait Brine. Unlike rock salt, pickling salt or kosher salt, Brine 'N Bite added several different advantages to traditional salt brines. Of course all salts will help toughen your baits, but Brine 'N Bite is loaded with a proprietary blend of complex amino acids that serve several purposes. Some of the amino acids used by Pro-Cure intensify the natural smell of the bait. Others break down the actual scent particles into smaller scent molecules so the natural scent of your herring travels further and faster through the water. And lastly, several of the amino acids we add were developed by the aquaculture industries to trigger an impulse in a salmon's brain to feed under stressed conditions. Needless to say, we've had this formula on the market for almost 20 years, and we've got top guides who buy it by the case just for their herring fishery. A year or two after that we introduced Bait Brite Bait Brightener. Basically it is a super concentrated laundry bluing product that has a chemical reaction with the scales on a herring or anchovy and produces a super bright, shiny bait. If I am fishing a natural bait I always add Bait Brite. If you are dealing with a herring shortage and are forced to use older bait that has started to yellow, eight hours in Brine 'N Bite Bait Brine with Bait Brite added should solve your problem. It is amazing, but your tired old baits will look like they were just harvested. Now your old baits will look nice and shiny, but their scent will smell old and

INJECTING A PLUG-CUT BAIT

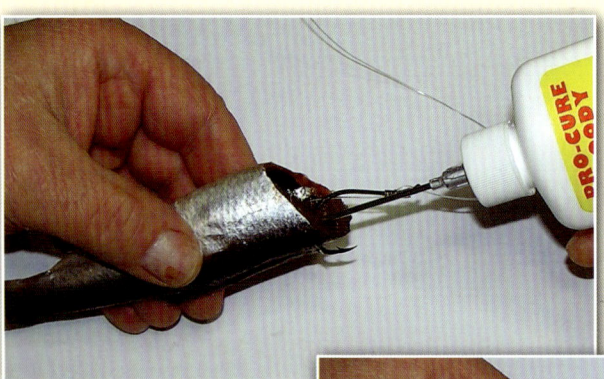

On either side of the spine push the needle down deeply into the bait's side, and then squeeze injector as you pull out.

Do this 2 to 3 times on either side of the spine. You can also put a few drops of oil into the body cavity.

stale once cut. This is offset by injecting your plug-cut baits with various Pro-Cure bait oils to overpower the old smell and attract biters. Lots of old-timers added powdered milk to their brines to add shine, and the lactose acid does put a shine on your baits, but it doesn't do nearly as good a job as bluing. Also, if you want to save your brine for a length of time the powdered milk may spoil or mold, and the bluing will not. Some anglers prefer to use laundry bluing they can buy at the

INJECTING A WHOLE BAIT

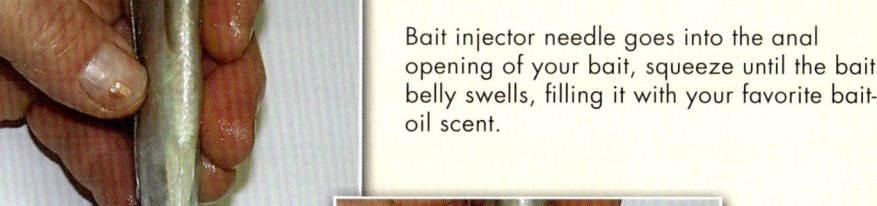

Bait injector needle goes into the anal opening of your bait, squeeze until the baits belly swells, filling it with your favorite bait-oil scent.

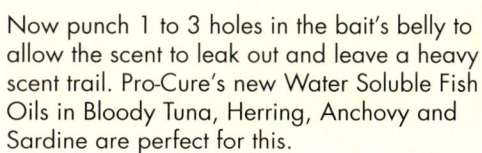

Now punch 1 to 3 holes in the bait's belly to allow the scent to leak out and leave a heavy scent trail. Pro-Cure's new Water Soluble Fish Oils in Bloody Tuna, Herring, Anchovy and Sardine are perfect for this.

Pro-Cure's newest, and possibly our biggest bait scent ever, Water Soluble Fish Oils are perfect for injecting into baits or adding to brine solutions to increase scent on baits. Water Soluble Fish Oils travel further and faster through the water column, and are much easier for a fish to pick up on than standard fish oils. All the Water Soluble Fish Oils are loaded with amino acids and UV flash. It's scent fish see as well as smell.

super market, but be careful to avoid any bluing products that have fragrances added. Lilac, Summer Breeze and Tropical Paradise will never become top salmon attractants, and may just be a top-shelf salmon repellant. So if your bluing is not fragrance-free play it safe and get some Pro-Cure Bait Brite.

Another major breakthrough in preparing world-class herring baits was the addition of Ultra-Violet enhancers. We call it UV flash. Fish, like birds and big-game animals, see UV with their natural eyesight. Humans eyes will not pick up the ultra-low-wave frequencies UV light travels at. But scientists now tell us they are convinced that salmon, and other species of fish actually find their prey by the natural UV reflection that comes off of the prey. This UV bounce comes off in sunlight, moonlight and star light, so except for the darkest cloud-covered night salmon are using ultra-violet light to find their prey. Several years ago Pro-Cure developed a product called Pure UV, and it is a unique liquid in the sense that it is both water and oil soluble. It mixes into both. So adding 8 to 10 drops of Pure UV Liquid into your brine solution will impregnate your baits with a reflective UV coating that will make your UV-treated baits stand out like light bulbs to a predator salmon. Not only will UV light penetrate down several hundred feet into the water column, it can be seen laterally up to 500 feet. This means when trolling a plug-cut herring 20 feet under the surface, a salmon might not see your herring from 80 feet away, but enhanced with the UV attractant that salmon may see your bait from 100 feet or more. The Pure UV Liquid is powerful, so it only takes 8 to 10 drops in two quarts of water to enhance your baits. Again it's one more product to give you an edge over the competition.

The lower herring was brined with Pure UV Liquid added to the brine. Salmon find their prey by the UV reflection that bounces off the prey. Adding UV flash, or using a product that already has it added, makes a huge difference.

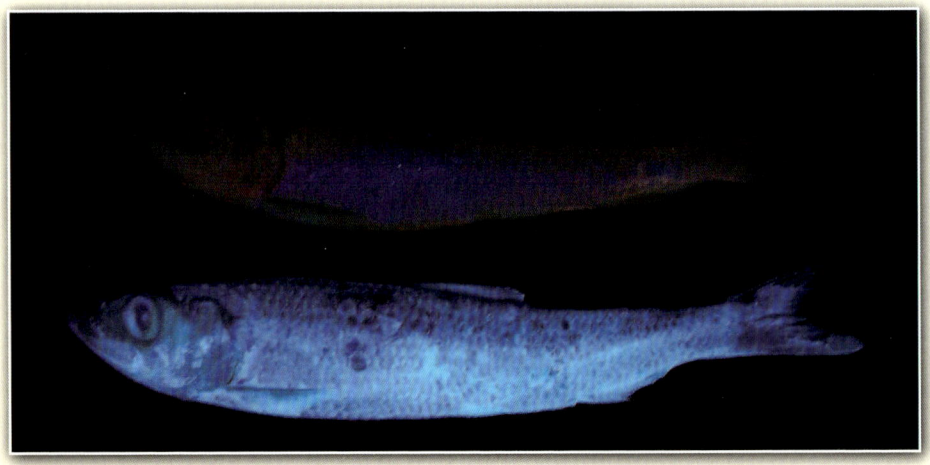

The full family of Pro-Cure products used for brining herring and anchovies.

If you've used Brine 'N Bite bait brine you have probably noticed that initially it's hard to get all the powder wet. Here's a little secret to make the whole process a lot more simple. I used to put all my powder into a plastic tray large enough to hold all of my brine and herring. I would then add my measured amount of water, and literally chase undissolved clumps of dry brine powder around the tray for 10 minutes or so. A more simple way is to put all of the powder into a 1-gallon freezer Ziplock bag. The brine formula calls for all the powder (20 ounces) and approximately two quarts of water. It's in a 22-ounce container, so after you pour the powder into the baggie, fill the container up to the top of the shoulder with good clean water. It can be well water, stream water, bay or ocean water. It should never be chlorinated city water, as the chlorine seems to repel fish. With your 20 ounces of water measured out, add just enough water to get all of the powder in the bag wet. Once the small amount of water is added, seal the bag and work the powder around, gently massaging the powder until it is all wet. Once completely wetted add the rest of the first container of water, fill the container two more times and add that to the baggie. Now gently massage it and work it around until all the powder is totally dissolved. Now pour your solution into a plastic tray large enough to handle the amount of herring you plan to brine, plus the brine solution. Make sure that if any wet powder remains in your baggie you shake it out into your bait tray. If I am planning on doing nice shiny natural baits I add 8 to 10 drops of Bait Brite to my solution, and 8 to 10 drops of Pure UV Liquid. Also, when adding my trayed herring I let them defrost only enough to slide off their foam packing tray without leaving scales frozen to the tray. If you tear frozen herring off the foam tray you will leave lots of scales stuck to the tray, and lost scales means less flash as your bait rolls. Unless it is extremely hot outside I let my bait tray sit at room temperature for 6 to 8 hours, or overnight. I never let my herring reach room temperature before I add them into my brine solution because once they warm up they rapidly start to deteriorate. I prefer to put them into brine as soon as they easily slide off the tray. If your herring are partially frozen when they go into the brine they are like little herring ice cubes, so they will significantly chill your brine solution. If you pack your brine tray in a cooler with ice you will get the water so cold because of the salt in the brine that your herring will stay frozen and will not absorb the curing salts and amino acids. Your bait needs to defrost while in the brine so it can absorb all the benefits of the brine. If you keep your bait frozen rock solid during the entire brine time you have accomplished nothing. Once the brining is complete (6 to 12 hours) it is IMPERATIVE to make sure your bait is iced in a cooler. Once brined, if you let your herring sit out in the sun and get warm they will quickly turn to mush and will not stay on your hooks. Even the best-brined baits can be ruined in 30 minutes or less if left out on a warm sunny day.

If you look inside a jar of the Brine 'N Bite powder, sometimes you'll notice the powder is very white, and other times it will have a tan or brownish color. The powder is extremely hydroscopic, so it rapidly attracts and absorbs moisture. The more moisture it attracts the more color it takes on, but whether it is white, tan or brown it is still the same brine powder. Some guides insist on using only the darkest brown powder as they feel it is stronger and works better, but it all starts out exactly the same. Inside a jar of Brine 'N Bite you'll find a usage chart which tells you how much powder-to-water to use if you are making smaller batches of brine. After many years of dealing with the powder we've come to the conclusion that making smaller batches is not a good idea because the powders we use are different weights and with shipping and handling the heavier salts tend to sink to the bottom of the jar, and the lighter amino acids float to the top, so in doing smaller batches you may not get the consistency you desire. What I recommend is doing the entire 20 ounces of powder in 60 to 64 ounces of pure water and then storing the unused liquid in a clean, lidded jar for as long as you want to store it. The pre-made liquid brine has an indefinite shelf life. In fact, if you pre-make all your brine all of the residual powder that is not normally dissolved is dissolved completely. Then you can use a pint, quart or all two quarts as you need it, and keep the balance stored until you need it again.

The next major breakthrough in plug-cut fishing came with the introduction of Bad Azz Bait Dyes in 6 hot fluorescent colors. This was about six or seven years ago, and the logic behind the dyes was simple. You don't fish one color of lure, plug, spoon, hoochie or flasher for salmon, so why fish one color bait? Right from the start Bad Azz dyes were a huge success, and they have literally changed how anglers fish herring. The most popular colors for herring have

A 41-pounds Chinook is a great reward for fishing plug-cut herring with a perfect roll. Big fish just can't resist a juicy piece of meat. I'll fish plug cut baits down to 80 feet.

been Chartreuse/Lime and Metallic Blue. Red, pink and orange are also popular spinner colors at Buoy 10, and some savvy guides have tried dying their herring these colors with excellent success. Here are a few tricks to help you if you plan on dying up some herring. I never add Bait Brite to my brine if I am planning on dying my herring, as it seems to interfere with the ability of the dyes to penetrate the herring. I still add Pure UV Liquid however. The powder dyes don't mix as easily in salted water as they do in fresh water, so I take about an ounce of fresh water and mix my dye powder separately from my pre-made brine solution, and then after my dye is mixed into plain water I add it to my brine solution. The powdered Bad Azz dyes are extremely concentrated, so to do 1 to 3 trays of Green label herring in Metallic Blue I usually add less than ¼ of a teaspoon of dye to my brine solution. Remember your baits are going to be brining from 6 to 12 hours, so if you get the color you want right away, in eight or more hours your bait will be too dark. If you start out a little light on the amount of dye you use, you can always add a little more dye a few hours into the brine time. Just remember to never (NEVER) sprinkle the dye powder directly into your brine solution. The dye does not initially dissolve well in heavily salted water, and it will clump up and make a mess. Always mix the dye with a little bit of fresh water first, and then add the dye solution to your brine mix.

Most folks think flat lining right behind the boat only works for silvers, but this Chinook was caught on a plug-cut herring with four ounces of lead, 6 pulls behind the boat. The flash and scent of a properly rolling plug-cut herring is hard to beat in any fishery.

When using the Bad Azz Chartreuse Lime color here's another little trick to get the brightest color baits. This color is not as strong as blue, red or purple, so I use about half a rounded teaspoon of dye, and a third of a rounded teaspoon of baking soda. The chartreuse dye is extremely pH sensitive, and by boosting the pH just a little bit makes the chartreuse color really pop. Conversely if you try to get a brighter chartreuse color by just adding more of the chartreuse dye it will actually 'muddy' the color, and you'll wind up with a flat, dull chartreuse mustard color. This doesn't mean if the color you are getting on your baits is not as strong as you'd like you shouldn't add more dye. Just add more dye in combination with more baking soda. Only use baking soda with the chartreuse dye. DO NOT add baking soda to any of the other dye colors. Another little trick is adding just a drop or two of the blue dye to your chartreuse dye solution. This will bring the color from the yellowish antifreeze chartreuse color towards a more fluorescent Kelly green. To do this, mix a tiny amount of the blue powder dye in water, and then add a few drops of the blue liquid to the chartreuse solution. You cannot add the blue dye powder directly to the chartreuse as the powder is too powerful to control, and you'll quickly wind up with a deep forest green.

Three years ago we introduced the Bad Azz Liquid dyes and they are great for doing small batches of bait, or spot dying individual baits. The Bad

Azz Liquid dyes already have UV flash added to the solution, so there is no need to add the Pure UV Liquid. Sometimes I'll rub the liquid chartreuse dye onto the front half of a few herring, so when I plug-cut them the first inch is chartreuse, just like a chrome/chartreuse Qwikfish. Also in the previous step where I talk about adding a small amount of blue dye powder to make a chartreuse solution a brighter green, a few drops of the blue liquid Bad Azz dye will do the trick perfectly.

Often I will take my brined natural herring onboard my boat in my brining container still in the brine liquid, but I never, ever take my dyed baits onboard in their dye solution. The chartreuse dye is fairly forgiving, and will clean up well on metal and plastic surfaces, but all of the other dye colors are extremely permanent. If you spill or splash the stain might be there forever. So before fishing I remove my baits from the dye solution, shake them off, and put them dry into a zip-lock baggie, or a clean bait tray. I also wear my Pro-Cure Ninja black nitrile gloves when handling the dyed baits to keep from dying my fingers. If you don't wear gloves, the good news is the dyes will eventually wear off, after a few days.

If it seems like there are a lot of steps to brining and dying baits, there are, but we just made life more simple by introducing Pro-Cure's newest addition, Brine 'N Bite COMPLETE Liquid Bait Brine. These are pre-mixed, ready-to-use liquid brines with dyes. We offer Natural Shine, which already has Bait Brite and Pure UV Liquid added, and it produces a beautiful, shiny bait that looks just harvested. If you are looking for convenience in dyed baits we offer Bait Brite Complete in Chartreuse Glow, Brilliant Blue and Magenta Red. All of the Complete liquids have UV Flash added and, most importantly, all have our blend of amino acids that make our brines so special. So if you're looking for convenience, and just want to do two or three trays of bait without all the mixing and measuring hassles, it doesn't get any easier than Brine 'N Bite COMPLETE.

Here's the newest addition to our great herring products: Brine 'N Bite Complete Liquid Brine. There's no mixing or measuring. Just add herring and you are ready to go. Brine 'N Bite Complete contains all the amino acids, as in in the powder Brine 'N Bite, plus it has UV flash added for extra fish attraction. And the dyes produce the most vibrantly color baits.

LEADER TYING/HOOK SIZES

I know I won't make any friends with the folks who sell pre-tied herring leaders, but I feel it is a must to tie your own leaders, or have someone custom tie them for you. When you purchase pre-tied leaders you cannot control leader pound test, the leader material they use, the quality of the material, hook sizes, and spacing between the hooks. As this article progresses you'll see just how important hook spacing and positioning is to creating successful rolls. On most leaders for plug-cut herring there are two hooks. The top hook controls the roll, and in most cases the bottom or trailing hook's sole purpose is hooking fish. It is critical to control the spacing between the hooks to maximize getting hooked up when a salmon strikes. Also, if you fish a pre-tied leader that's hook spacing is correct for a Green label herring, the hook's spacing will be way too short for the larger Blue baits. Conversely a pre-tied leader for Blue label herring will not be good for a Green label bait. The pound test your leader is tied on and the hook sizes can negatively affect your rolls. The lightest leader you can get away with will allow you a faster roll, as long as the pound test is adequate to handle larger fish. And hooks proportionate to the bait size will also give you a faster roll. On a regularly sized Green label herring I usually use two 3/0 octopus hooks, or a 3/0 on my trailing hook and a 4/0 on my top hook. On a large Blue label herring I may use a 6/0 for my top hook, and a 4/0 or 5/0 for the trailing hook. If you have a store-bought pre-tied leader with two 3/0 hooks, and you're rigging a Blue label herring, the hooks are too small and don't have enough hook point sticking out through your bait to provide adequate hooking power. Conversely two 5/0 hooks are too large for a Green label herring, and using them will significantly slow down your roll. Another reason to avoid pre-tied leaders is the material the leader is tied on. In areas where the fish are really leader shy many guides are tying their leaders on fluorocarbon material, or a fluorocarbon mono hybrid material, rather than standard monofilament material. Supposedly fluorocarbon material is completely invisible underwater, and some guides swear it's responsible for a few more bites on the tough days. I've become really fond of the P-Line fluorocarbon material, but there are lots of other quality brands out there. Talking about brands, always use quality hooks. Over the years I have become extremely fond of Gamakatsu hooks. They have never failed me, and I have an excellent hook-up ratio. But nowadays there are many top-quality hooks on the market, and one I am growing extremely fond of is Eagle Claw's new Trokar hooks. I got to fish a few sample packs last summer and they are hot. Another thing I like about the Trokar hooks – they are made in the good ol' USA.

Lots of guys are intimidated when it comes to tying knots, or are just too lazy or disorganized to tie their leaders in advance. It only takes learning one or two knots to tie the best custom herring leaders, and you really need to learn them. You may be at a huge disadvantage if relying on pre-tied leaders. If I'm

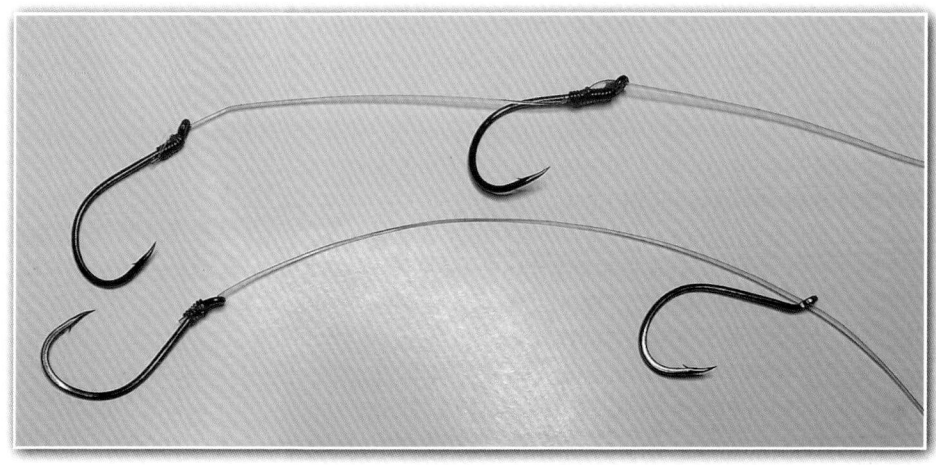

Traditional plug-cut rigs require two hooks, but it is only the top hook that controls the roll. The bottom hook's sole purpose is to hook biting salmon. On most rolls you could clip off the bottom, trailing hook and get exactly the same roll.

watching a movie or sporting event I'll tie my leaders in bulk and store them on a piece of hollow foam insulation tubing. If you tie in advance make sure you are positive about your hook spacing, and then label your rolls. For example on a piece of masking tape I'll have written "Green label, 7' 30# 4/0 3/0." If I plan on fishing Blues or Purples I will tie up leaders with different spacing, larger hooks, and possibly on 40- or 50-pound material. Not having your leaders pre tied is unacceptable, and may cost you fish. If you find yourself in the middle of a red-hot bite, and you've just landed a double and it's got all four of your lines in a tangled mess, the last thing you want to be doing is tying new herring leaders. Just snip off or unclip the mess, re-clip your pre-tied droppers and leaders, and in a minute or so you are back to fishing. When you land a fish always check your leader for nicks and abrasions. Knowingly fishing a damaged leader because you don't want to have to re tie another whole leader is a recipe for disaster. When you see a bad spot and rationalize it's good enough for one more 12-pound springer, that's when the fish of your season, in the high thirties, will hit and 10 feet from the net pop you off, right at the bad spot you knew about. Don't risk it. Have a good supply of pre-tied leaders with you.

As I mentioned, the top hook, and its placement, controls the diameter of the roll. In almost all cases the trailing hook is added to improve your chances of hooking up. Just for giggles rig a plug-cut bait with your two hooks and observe the roll really close to your boat. Now snip off the bottom hook right below the top hook's snell. Put the bait back in the water and you will have the exact same roll. The trailing hook has nothing to do with the roll you get. Only the placement of your top hook controls the roll.

When we filmed the tying of herring leaders for our 'how to' DVD I used an egg loop bumper knot for both the trailing hook and the top hook. In actuality you can use any type of knot on the trailing hook. It can be an egg loop bumper knot, an improved clinch knot, a Trilene knot, or even a Palomar knot. When tying on a lure or spinner I usually leave the knot's tag long, but it is imperative on the lower trailing hook to clip the tag as close to the knot as possible, especially if you are passing this trailing hook through the meat of the bait. A longer tag will tear up baits as you work the hook through the bait's flesh, especially in an area right above the tail, where there is not a lot of meat. I used to use a small nailclipper to clip my tags close, but of late I have become attached to the new Boomerang clippers on the retractable lanyard. It clips the tag really close, and I have attached mine to the top of my bibs to always have them handy.

I mentioned spacing between the hooks, and this is determined by the size of the baits, and where you want the two hooks placed on your bait. If you are pre-tying leaders in advance of going fishing take out a tray of frozen bait and lay your top hook on top of the imaginary plug-cut line right behind the bait's gill cover. This should give you your spacing. If unsure, tie up a test leader and see where your test hooks position out. If you're not sure of the distance between hooks you might want to sacrifice one bait to check out precise distances before tying up a bunch of leaders. If you have a work bench you can make your hook spacing marks on the bench, but if not I measure hook spacing with my fingers. It's not exact, but close enough, and you always have your fingers with you, so you may choose to run a 3/0 hook as your trailer, and

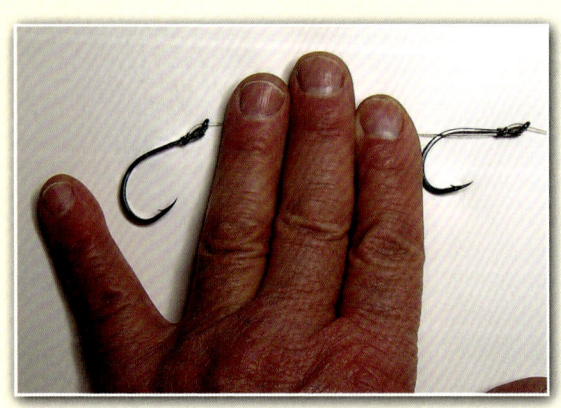

a 4/0 hook as the top hook, with 3 fingers spacing between the hooks. Once I am ABSOLUTELY SURE of my hook spacing I tie up at least a dozen leaders in advance. If I get into a tangle, or land a fish and my leader is nicked, the last thing you want during a hot bite is to be retying a leader. Especially a leader with two snelled hooks. Also, when I tie my leaders I almost always pull off at least 6 feet of leader material. I can always cut it shorter if I don't need it, but if you get into a really picky bite, or the fish seem leader shy, and you need long leaders, tying on an add-on piece is a real pain. Plus, the more knots you have building a leader, the more chances of a knot failing.

I know a lot of anglers are intimidated tying anything besides basic knots, but our new Pro-Cure DVD on plug-cutting offers something a little different. About halfway through filming all of the 'how to' for knot tying and rigging plug-cut I realized that I was being filmed face on. The camera was facing me. That means you as the viewer would see everything you had to do backwards, and have to reverse it in your mind to make it work. So we scrapped a whole bunch of great 'how to' footage, and re shot it all with the camera placed over my left shoulder. This camera angle gives viewers a clear look at exactly how to tie the knots from their perspective! With that in mind we will show you here all the knot-tying steps with the camera over my shoulder so you can see each step as you would see it as you tie it.

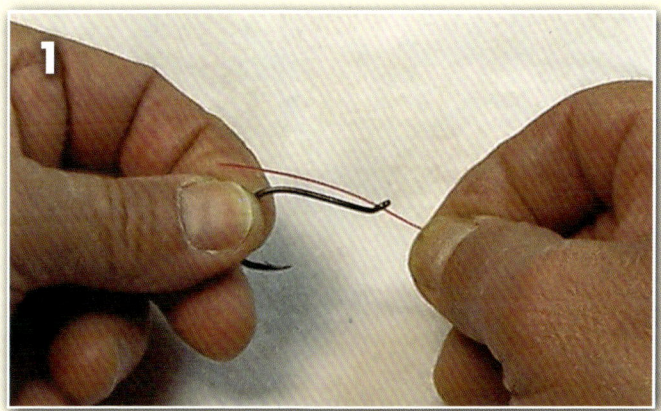

Place leader end through eye of trailing hook about 1/2 inch past hook bend.

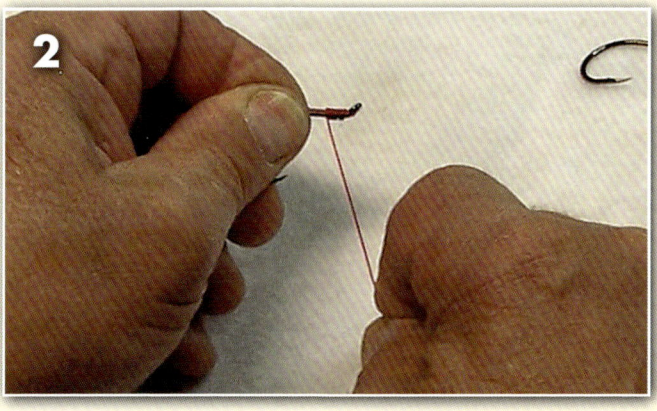

Wrap leader tightly around and behind hook eye and make 5 to 7 tight turns around the hook shank towards the rear of the hook.

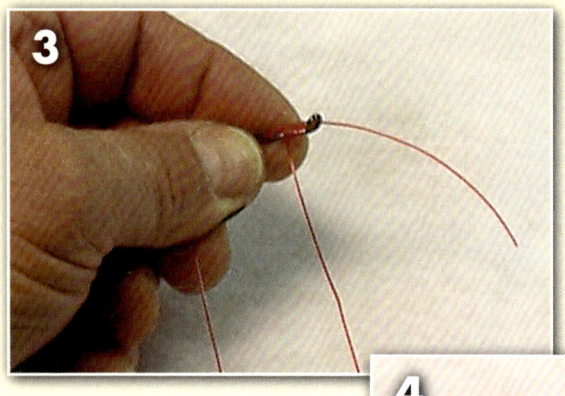

Use your index finger to hold the wraps in place against the hook shank and then pass the opposite end of the leader through the hook eye. Then make 4 to 6 more wraps around the hook shank towards the rear of the hook. Hold both wraps in place with your index finger, wet the leader and pull all of it through both knots. Then use your scissor handle to pull the top knot up tight.

Pull the knot up tightly until the tag pops under the wrap turns. Make sure it locks in place or the knot will unravel. The finger holes in a scissor works great for this.

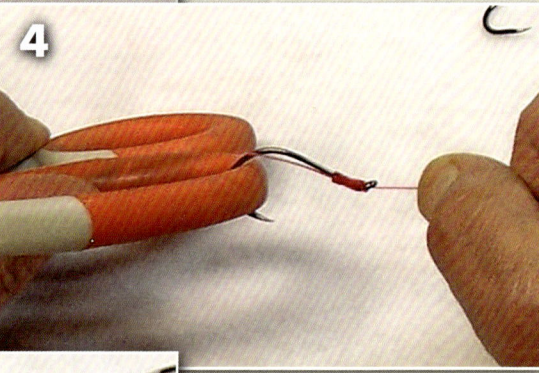

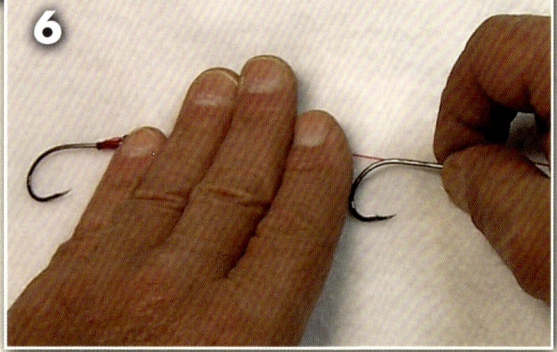

If you plan on passing the hooks through your bait's body make sure you clip the tag end close to the knot to avoid tearing up the meat of the bait when you pass the hook through.

Use your fingers or a mark to measure the space between the trailing hook and the top hook. If unsure, try a tied leader on one of your baits. If the spacing is correct then tie up a bunch of leaders.

A finished leader ready to be stored. I usually label my pre-tied leaders by pound test, leader length, hook sizes and what size baits they are tied for. Example: 30#, 6', 4/0, 3/0 Green label.

PLUG-CUT ROLLS

Most plug-cut rolls are done with a compound cut, or two angles in the same cut. The angle of how you cut the bait is one of the variables that control the roll of your bait. In fact there are basically three variables that control the roll of your bait. The first is the angle of the cut, the second is the placement of the hooks, and the third is the troll speed or current speed.

One of the easiest ways to eliminate one variable is to use a plug-cutting tool to add more consistency to your rolls. Several companies offer plug-cutting tools, from cheap injection-molded plastics to heavy-duty aluminum tools. Basically a plug-cutter is a miter box that you place your herring into, and there are offset slots that guide your knife while cutting your bait. The knife guides give you the exact same compound angle cut every time. The exact angle eliminates one of the variables to getting consistent rolls on your bait. When you hand-cut baits the angles can change, and you will notice at one speed one or two of your cut baits are rolling perfectly, and one or two are not. Speed your boat up, and the two rolls that were struggling become perfect, and the two good ones begin to mess up. So for consistency a plug-cutter tool is recommended. There are several benefits to using the Pro-Cure Precision Cutter. Firstly the compound angles were designed by Gary Gilchrist and they produce great rolls. Our cutter is heavy-duty anodized aluminum with a UMHW riveted plastic insert the whole length of the cutter to make sure your plug-cut knife doesn't get dull cutting on bare aluminum. It is wide enough to lay a Green, Blue, Purple or Black label herring into. Some cutters on the market will not handle a bait larger than a Green label herring. Short of dropping it overboard or running it over the Pro-Cure Precision Cutter should last you a lifetime.

Although Green label herring is the most common plug-cut bait size, the plug-cutter you choose should be able to handle the larger baits like Purples (shown here) and Blacks.

Using a plug-cut tool will give you more consistent angles than hand-cutting a herring.

Of course there are some rolls that require cutting by hand. Some have a very flat cut, and some require a very severe angled cut. We'll cover some of the custom rolls, and how to fine-tune your rolls by adjusting cut angles. It's funny, but 20 years ago lots of folks were looking for big, slow rolls. Ideally your herring would be rolling in a large 4- to 6-inch circle. Now top guides and anglers are looking for extremely tight, super fast rolls that almost resemble a spinner blade with their flash. Almost all of this is controlled by hook placement. When you plug-cut a herring it's pretty standard to remove all the internal organs (or guts.) It only takes a second or two, and usually results in a more consistent roll. If you place a plug-cut herring facing you, with the body cavity opening facing you, you'll notice that right above the cavity is the bait's spine. The flesh of a baitfish is fairly soft, but the spine is tough. So when rigging herring you want to make sure your top hook is always going through the spine. It can go through from the right to the left, or the opposite. As long as the hook goes through the

ADVANCED TECHNIQUES FOR PLUG-CUT HERRING

Top: Traditional cut-plug angle using a Pro-Cure Killer Kutter. **Middle:** A severe hand-cut will generate faster rolls. **Bottom:** An extremely flat hand-cut. As you can see there is lots of room for slightly different variations of compound angles you can cut by hand, and although there is a time and a purpose for all these different cuts, every different plug-cut angle will give your baits a different roll. If you hand-cut without precise consistency you will never get a consistent, fish-catching roll. This is why many top guides rely on a plug-cutting tool.

spine! This is the toughest part of the bait and in most cases, it will help keep your hook from tearing out of your bait. Again, looking at your cut bait, picture the spine as the 12 o'clock position on a clock, and then going clockwise, visualizing the 1, 2 and 3 o'clock positions on your bait. The 3 o'clock position is right about at the bait's lateral line, and it's about as low as you want to position your hook. The closer your hook is to the 12 o'clock position will give you the very tightest rolls. The more you bring your hook towards 3 o'clock the larger your rolls will become. So for a super-tight roll your hook can go into the cavity and through the spine from the left side, and up and through the spine to come out at 12:15, 12:30 or 1 o'clock. Or it could start at the right side of the spine and come out at the 11:45, 11:30 or the 10 o'clock position. Either way you should get the same, super-tight rolls.

If you imagine the herring's spine as 12 o'clock, and the positions to the right as 1, 2 and 3 o'clock, and the positions to the left of the spine as 11, 10 and 9 O'clock, these are the positions that you want your top hook to come out through. The angle of the cut, plus the positioning of the top hook will control the tightness and speed of the roll. The positions between 11 and 1 O'clock, closest to the spine, will give you the tightest, fastest rolls. The more you move your hook down the bait's sides, towards 9 or 3 O'clock, will give you the larger, slower rolls.

Another mistake I constantly see is rolls that tail flop. A tail flop is where the front of the herring is rolling in a 2-inch circumference, and the tail is rolling in a 5- or 6-inch circumference. This tail-flop roll might work on ocean Coho during a red hot bite, but Chinook usually do not prefer this type of roll. Many years ago I was making the same mistake, and constantly had rolls that tail-flopped. Finally a guide buddy took me under his wing and showed me my mistake. I was so afraid my baits would tear off I was burying my top hook too deeply inside the bait's cavity, figuring the more meat between the edge of the plug-cut and the hook the longer my bait would stay on. This was not only wrong, but when you bury your top hook deep inside a bait's cavity you create a hinge point, because there is so much of the bait in front of the hook that current pushes the forward edge of the bait sideways, so as it rolls the front rolls in a 1- to 2-inch circle, and the tail rolls in a huge 4- to 6-inch circle. In most current conditions running your top hook through the bait's spine, rather than setting it too deeply into the bait's body cavity will solve the tail-flop problem. If you picture your bait rolling through a clear plastic tube about 2 inches in diameter, neither the head nor the tail should be touching the wall of the tube.

After you've plug-cut your bait, if you set it on its belly, with its dorsal fin pointing straight up, and you look down on your bait from directly above, you will notice one side of the cut bait is longer than the other. So one side is called the short side, and the other side the tall side. Anglers always tell me they can never remember which side of the bait the trailing hook and top hook go through. Surprise! It doesn't matter. Whether you run your trailing hook through the short side, and your top hook

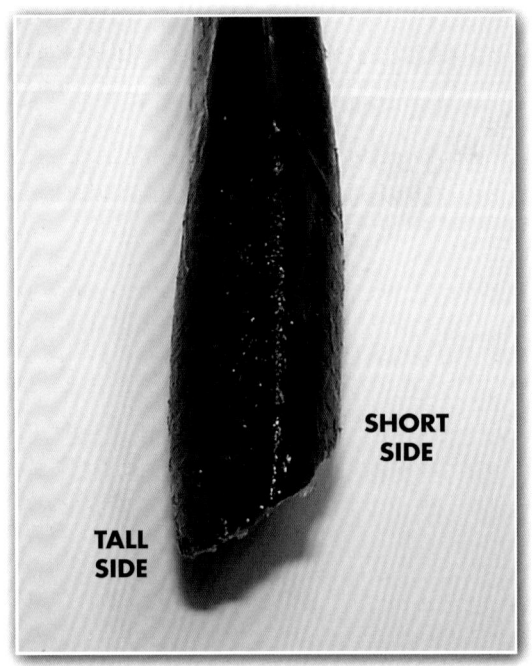

SHORT SIDE

TALL SIDE

After plug-cutting a bait you will have a tall side and a short side of the bait. That's what we will reference when explaining hook placement.

ADVANCED TECHNIQUES FOR PLUG-CUT HERRING

through the spine from right to left and come out at 11 o'clock, or run the trailing hook through the tall side, and run the top hook through the spine from left to right and come out at the 1 o'clock position you will basically have the same roll.

So assuming we are now placing our top hook correctly, and getting good tight rolls, the next item to discuss is where to place the second hook to get more hook-ups. Let's face it, you've got your rolls figured out, and you're finally getting bit, and now your hook-up percentage is less than 50%. If you are fishing Coho in the ocean, and are getting 20-plus hits a day, a 50% hook-up is livable. But if your up on the Columbia River, and a good day is 4 to 6 strikes, 50% might leave your fish box looking pretty empty. So there are ways to place your second hook (the trailing hook) that can greatly increase your hook-up ratio. We'll even cover rigging a herring with three hooks that virtually eliminates missing the short biters.

Many guides run their trailing hook through the side of the bait at the lateral line, and just let the trailing hook dangle at that point. Or they may not run the trailing hook through the bait at all, they just set the top hook and start to fish. The distance between the top hook and the trailing hook may vary considerably. But no matter the distance between both hooks there is a disadvantage to rigging this way, it leaves a large part of your bait exposed to a strike, without a hook in it. Not only will you miss short biters when rigged this way, but as your bait rolls, especially with the lighter pound test leaders (20-, 25-pound), the centrifugal force of the spinning bait will throw the trailing hook out away from your bait. Your bait may be spinning in a 1- to 2-inch circle, and your trailing hook can be spinning in a 4- to 6-inch circle. Depending on the angle an attacking salmon comes in from, it can swallow almost three quarters of your bait without coming close to a hook. In some fisheries biters are too scarce to be wasted by careless rigging. Once you have your leaders tied correctly it only takes an extra second or two to rig the trailing hook properly. I usually prefer burying the trailing hook in the side of my bait at least three quarters of the way down its side.

Another trick I use to deal with tail biters is to leave enough space between my trailing hook and my top hook to be able to work my trailing hook carefully through the meat just above the tail, and have my trailing hook completely exposed right on top of the tail. The amount of exposed leader is so negligible that the hook stays right up against the tail. It's easy to rig this way, and it really cuts down on missed fish.

Getting hooked up! It's not enough to get bit. You need to get bit and get hooked up. That's why placement of the second, or trailing, hook is so critical. Here are a few options for the famed Westport Roll, with your trailing hook in different positions.

Westport Roll: With trailing hook left outside the body cavity. As you can see this hook-up is quick and easy, but it leaves a whole lot of your herring unprotected with short biters. You can leave more distance between the two hooks, to get your tailing hook closer to the tail, but on a fast roll centrifugal force will have the trailing hook swinging out way away from your herring, leaving much of it unprotected.

Westport Roll: With the trailing hook outside the body cavity, and partially buried into the side of the hook. This style also leaves a whole lot of your herring unprotected from short biters.

Westport Roll: With trailing hook through the body cavity, out the tall side, and buried closer to the tail. I like this set-up for fairly aggressive biters, as the trailing hook is close enough to the tail to get most of the short biters. Again the trailing hook can be run outside the body cavity, or through the body cavity before burying it close to the tail.

Westport Roll: With trailing hook buried just above the tail. I use this set-up a lot for ocean Coho, as many fish seem to specialize in tail nipping baits.

Westport Roll: Another option I use a lot for ocean Coho is to run my trailing hook carefully through the meat just above the tail, and let my hook trail about a half to one inch behind the tail. By running the hook through the meat it will keep the trailing hook in close proximity to the tail. If you run your leader down that far, or beyond the tail, and let it dangle loose, as your bait rolls the centrifugal force can throw your trailing hook out and away from your bait. Your bait may be rolling in a 2-inch circle, but your trailing hook may be doing an 8-inch circle. With your hook far away from your bait you can see how much of it can be totally unprotected.

These five options to rigging a trailing hook on a Westport Roll show how important hook spacing is. If you cannot tie your own leaders you will never be able to maximize your strike-to-hook-up ratio.

THREE-HOOK RIG

Another way to give your herring maximum hook protection is to use a three-hook rig. Tying the leader with three hooks is more time consuming, and so is rigging your bait. The three-hook rig is not hard to do, it just takes more time. But on tough days, when biters are scarce, it is often worth the extra effort. It places a hook for tail biters, one mid section, and one at the bait's head. Even though the occasional fish will miss on this rig, missed strikes are a rarity.

Three-Hook Set-Up: If I am still getting short bit, or missing a lot of strikes, I will resort to rigging my baits with 3 hooks. It's a bit of extra work to tie my leaders and rig my baits, but on days when 3 to 5 strikes is considered good, how many do you want to miss?

Tied 3-hook leader. Spacing between hooks can vary depending on hook placement.

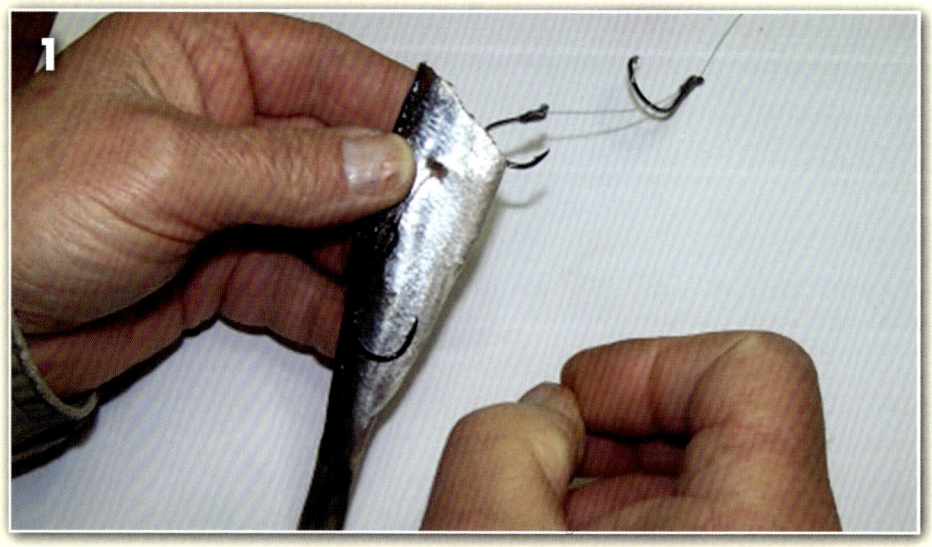

Go deeply into body cavity on tall side of bait,
work hook out through the side on the lateral line.

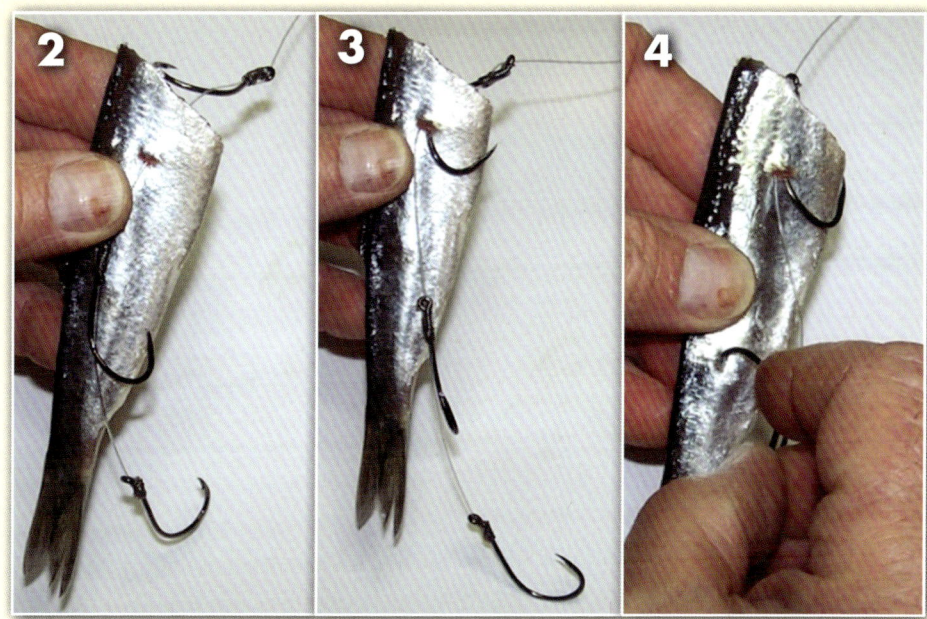

Work middle hook through same hole and then bring top hook (third hook) partially through the same hole to give yourself slack to work with. After bottom two hooks are positioned, the top hook is brought out through the same hole and properly positioned to give you the roll you want.

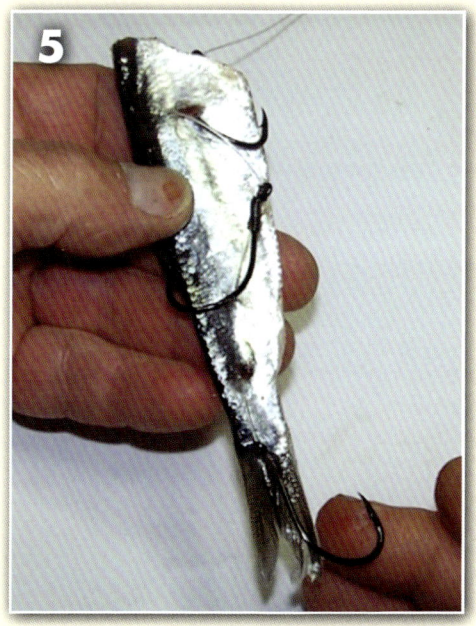

Carefully work the trailing hook through the meat and then work the middle hook partially through the same hole, lay the hook on its side and pull it UNDER the skin. Then push the hook eye up along the spine to lock the middle hook in place.

Three-Hook Rig

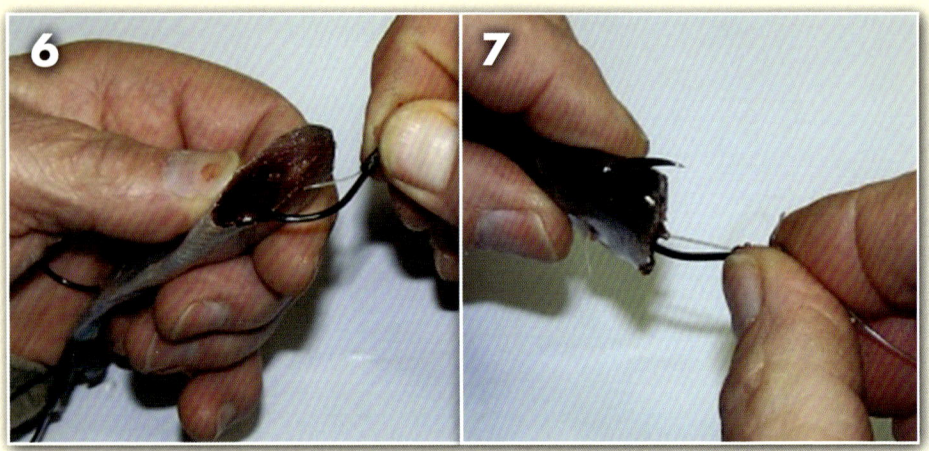

Pull the top hook back through the side hole and without going too deeply into the bait's body cavity work the hook point through the spine, starting left of the spine, through the spine, and out at the 12:15 to 1 o'clock position.

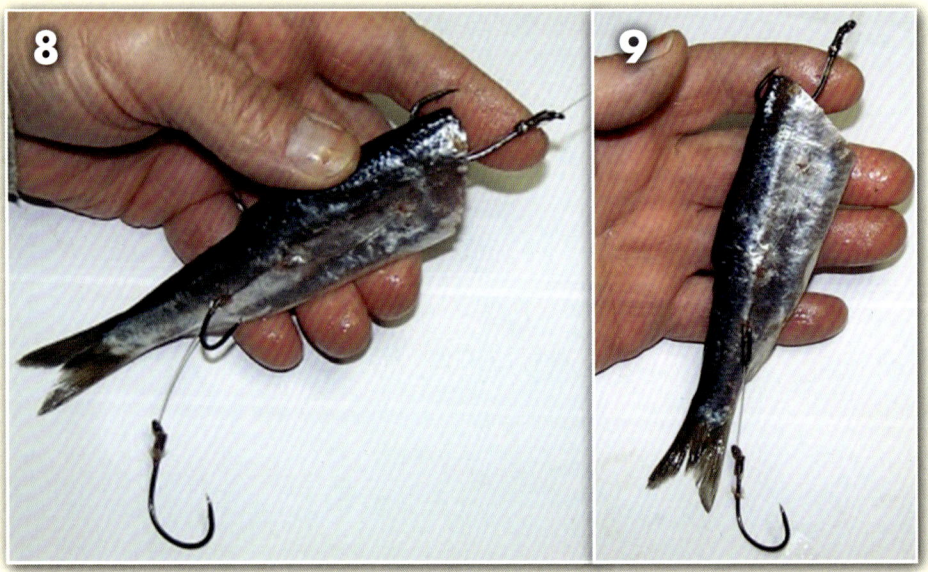

Two views of the 3-hook rig. With the top hook at the 12 to 1 o'clock position you will get a very fast roll, and virtually all of your bait is protected by a hook.

Cutting Vents

Cutting vents in herring relieves some of the pressure on your bait when trolling at faster speeds, or trolling against heavy current. I have to be honest, there are many times I don't cut a vent. If my bait is rolling at the speed I want it to roll, and not tearing off, why waste the time? But when cutting a vent there are two ways to do it. One is to insert a sharp knife up the fish's anal vent, and slit the belly from the vent up to the ventral fins on the belly. Another technique is to cut the herring at an angle, sideways, from the anal vent just to the spine, making sure you don't cut through the spine. This also allows the water flow to pass through the body cavity, and reduces the current's pressure on your bait.

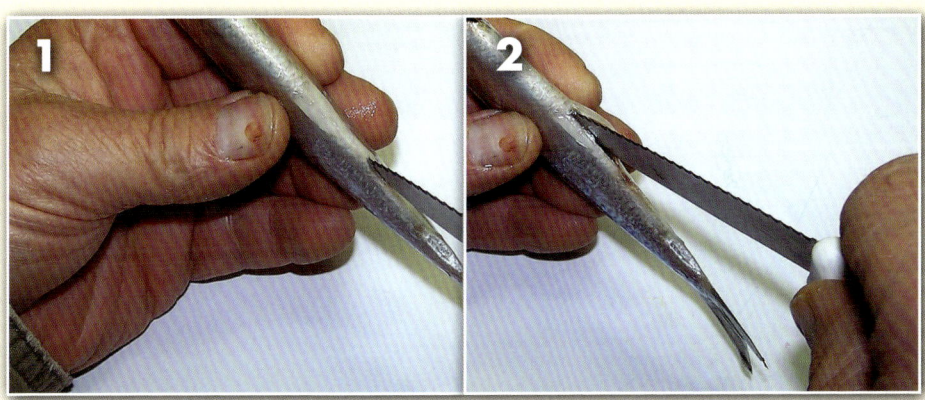

Option 1: Using a sharp knife, enter bait's anal opening
and carefully work up bait until you reach its anal fins.
At this point the opening will allow water to flow through the bait's body cavity.

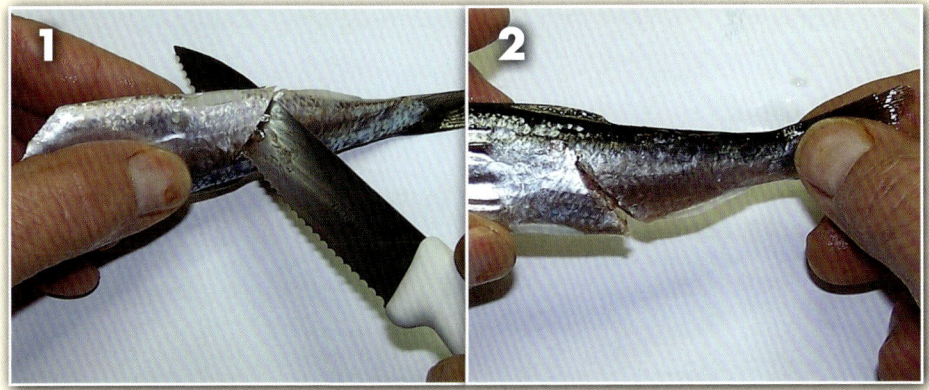

Option 2: Start cut at anal vent and, on a slant, work blade down to spine but not through it. Like the belly slit, this vent style allows water to pass through your bait, and reduces roll speed and pressure if your baits are tearing off.

BURYING A HOOK

It may take you ruining a bait or two to get this figured out, but if it's done right it almost feels like there is a little compartment your hook eye and hook shank slides up into, and locks in place, with just part of the bend and hook point showing. When burying a hook, work the hook point steeply and deeply into the bait's side, and then carefully work the hook point around and out the side of your bait. Now carefully work the hook shank out the same hole, but right before you work the hook eye and snell through the entrance hole lay the hook over on its side and it will pull through your bait without tearing it up. One of the mistakes I initially made when I tried burying a hook was going through the side of my baits way too shallowly. You don't want your hook point to go through the opposite side of your baits, but you want it in deeply enough to feel the spine as you work the hook point around and out through the side. If it's done right you'll be amazed how durable your bait will be when rigged this way. In many instances you will pull your trailing hook through first, and then bury the top hook into the same hole. This is why I have you cutting off the tag end of the trailing hook so closely. If you leave it long it will tear up your baits as you work it through the sides, especially with the heavier pound test leaders.

BURYING A HOOK (Steps 1-2) AND RIGGING A WESTPORT ROLL

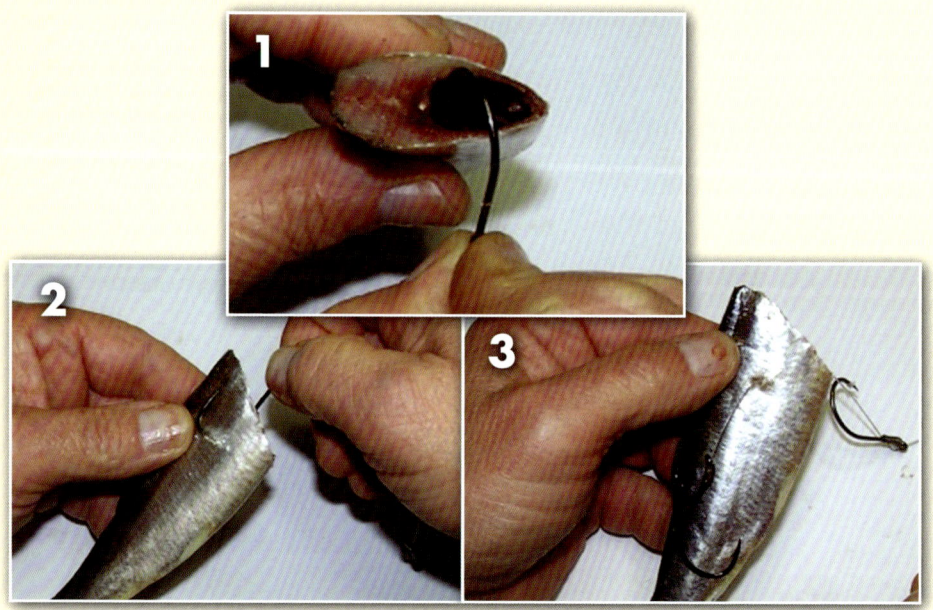

Work trailing hook deeply into the body cavity and carefully out the tall side of your bait. Now work the top hook out the same side. Or through enough to give yourself slack to place the trailing hook where you want it.

THE WESTPORT ROLL AND BURYING A TRAILING HOOK

There are many different herring rolls, and many variations from those rolls. One of the most well used, or most standard, is the Westport Roll. This roll, or a variation of it, is probably used by 90 percent of the top plug-cut anglers 80 to 90 percent of the time. It can be hand-cut, or cut using a plug-cutter. The top of the bait is cut at a compound angle, and the guts removed. If you look from the top of the bait down, you will have a tall side and a short side. A two-hook leader is the standard way to rig this cut. Pass your trailing hook through the tall side of the bait, at about the lateral line, and as deeply into the bait's body cavity as you can work the hook. As we discussed earlier, at this point you can let the trailing hook dangle freely, or bury the hook into the side of the bait. If I'm in a super hot ocean bite I may let the trailing hook dangle to save time, but usually I prefer to bury the trailing hook about three quarters of the way down the bait's side. If burying the hook, and you find you haven't left quite enough line between your top hook and trailer, pass the top hook through the same hole you worked your trailing hook through. This will give you plenty of slack to bury the trailing hook, and then pass the top hook back out the same hole, and, without going too deeply into the body cavity of the bait, carefully work the hook through the spine, from the tall side, through the spine, at anywhere from the 12:15 position, all the way down to the 3 o'clock position. Remember the closer you are to the 12 o'clock position, the tighter the roll you will get.

Now bury the trailing hook at least halfway down the bait's tall side and carefully work the trailing hook through the bait's side.

This rigging can also be reversed, running the trailing hook through the short side of your bait, and then carefully working your top hook from the short side of your bait, through the spine, so the hook point comes out the tall side of your bait, anywhere from the 11:45 position to the 9 o'clock position. Although the sides are reversed, the roll is basically the same. With the top hook on either side of the spine it doesn't change the roll much.

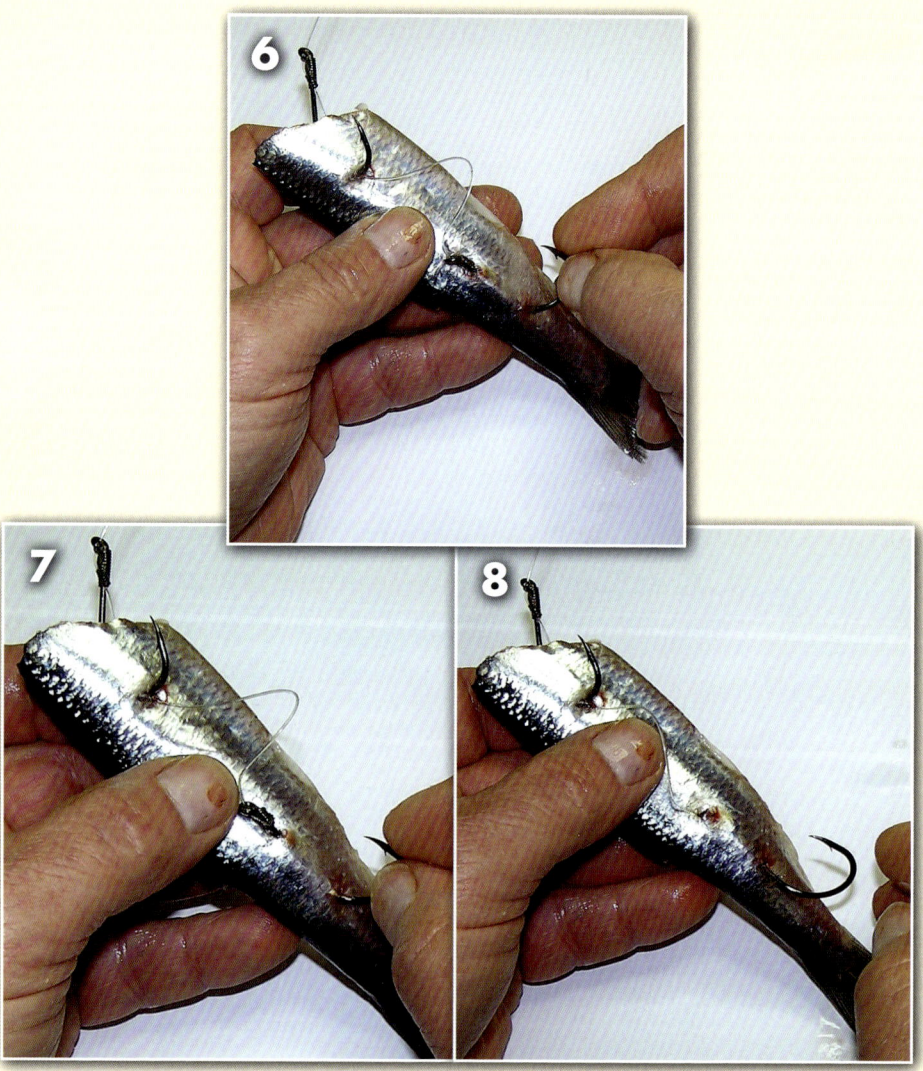

Work the hook's shank through the bait's side until you come to the eye and the snell. Now roll the hook over on its side and pull it through until the hook eye goes under the bait's skin, but not all the way through and out the hole.

ADVANCED TECHNIQUES FOR PLUG-CUT HERRING

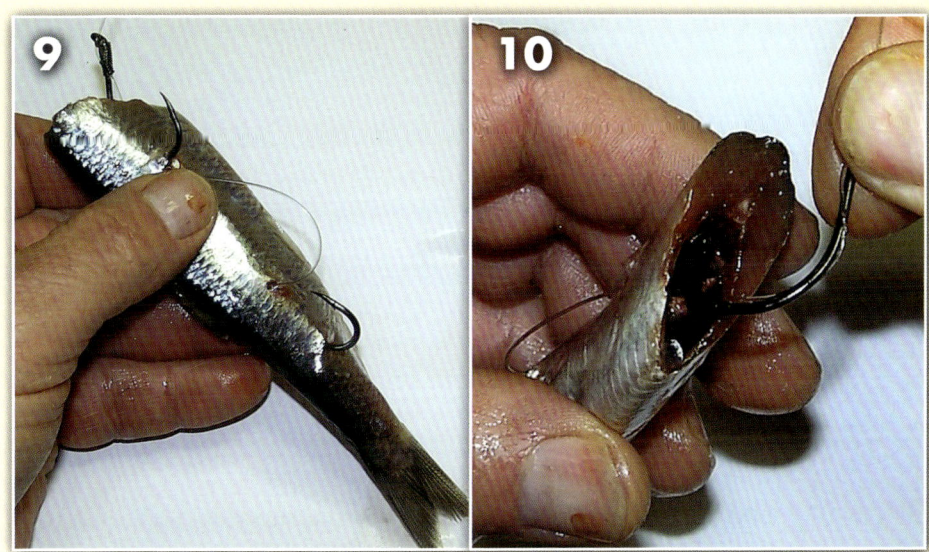

Now push the hook eye up along the baits spine, until you feel it 'lock' into place. Now your hook is properly buried into your baits side. Now work the top hook back out the top hole.

Without going too deeply into the body cavity work the hook point through the baits spine from the left side, through the right side, to come out at the 12:30 to 1 o'clock position. If you want a slower, larger roll work the hook point out through the 2 or 3 o'clock position.

Top view of your rigged herring. With the top hook placement at near the 12 o'clock position this is a very tight, fast Westport Roll. Also note how close to the cut edge the top hook is placed. Because this hook goes through the bait's spine it will stay on for all but the fastest troll. Again if this top hook is set too deeply into the bait's cavity it will create a 'hinge' point and you will get a tail-flop roll.

A TRUE REVERSE ROLL

One of my old guide buddies from Wenatchee, Washington, is a left-hander, and he hand-cuts his herring in a reverse of what most plug-cutting tools do, or for that matter what most hand-cutters do. Most anglers, and with most plug-cutting tools, the bait is laid into the cutter with the tail pointing to the left, and the head pointing to the right. The compound angle cut is then made right behind gill plate, with the top of the cut slanting slightly back towards the tail, and at an angle where the cut is closer to the gill plate on the top side of the bait than the bottom side. This is the standard cut almost all plug-cut anglers use. With the reverse roll, the roll is basically the same speed as a regular roll, and it too is controlled by the placement of the top hook, but the roll is reversed. Instead of rolling clockwise, it rolls counter clockwise. Two things happen here. One is the roll is a little different, and it's possible that that difference may catch a fish's attention, especially in a highly competitive fishery, where a fish is seeing lots of plug-cut baits dragged in front of it. The biggest difference is where the sun is positioned, and if you are getting more flash from a bait rolling clockwise versus counterclockwise. I've cut and rigged baits from both sides, and trolled them side by side, and there is a difference on the amount of flash the rolls put out. I am not suggesting we get so anal that we cut our baits one way when trolling right to left, and another way left to right. All I am saying is some days I'll do a lefty cut, and it pays off. Not always, but enough times to give a lefty bait a try for 30 minutes or so.

COVERING MORE WATER,
AND THE ROLLS THAT ALLOW YOU TO DO SO

If you are in a spot where the fish are stacked in front of your baits, the last thing you want to do is troll away from biting fish. You want to control your boat speed to sit right on top of that group of fish, but while doing this you need your rolls to perform. You may have to change your cut angles or hook placement to do this. Conversely if you are dealing with fish scattered throughout a river or a bay, or scattered over a wide area in the ocean, the last thing you want is to be trolling in one spot. You want to be moving to put your baits in front of fish, and hopefully find a biter or two. Now I know sometimes boat traffic and direction of that traffic dictates how you have to fish, but if, let's say you have a landmark you can see, and thirty minutes later you haven't moved 10 feet, and no one around you is getting bit, why stay there? If fish are scattered you have to move to cover more water. If to do this you are traveling downstream, with the current, you may think you're traveling fast enough to be water skiing, but boat versus land speed doesn't matter. Just make sure the speed you are at has your baits rolling well. If you're traveling with the currents, and your baits are barely rolling, you need to speed up. Again, don't worry about your ground speed, just predicate your boat speed on how well your baits are rolling.

If you need to cover more ground, and are forced to go against ocean current, tide or river current, you may need a way to rig that allows your bait to stay on in extremely heavy current. If your baits are getting ripped off your hooks in just a minute or two it makes no sense to be trolling empty hooks. So we'll discuss several different ways to deal with high troll speeds or heavy currents. A simple way to make a slight improvement on wildy spinning baits is to cut vents into your baits, or cut the angle of your baits flatter to reduce roll speed. If your baits keep tearing off I suggest two rolls to try. One roll I call the Gilly Roll because Gilly showed it to me years ago, and the other is rolling a whole herring.

THE GILLY ROLL

The Gilly Roll is a very durable plug-cut roll that will allow you to troll at faster trolling speeds, and cover more water. After plug-cutting your bait in your plug-cutter and removing the guts, run both hooks through the short side of your bait as deeply into the body cavity as you can get, and then run both hooks out the side of your bait, on the lateral line, through the same hole. Bring both hooks over the bait's back to the tall side of the bait, and then work the trailing hook deeply into the bait on the lateral line about 1 inch behind the tall-side cut. Carefully work the entire hook through the flesh, laying the hook on its side as you pull it through the flesh. You must work the hook point deeply into the flesh or it will tear out. Then work the top hook into the same hole, lay the hook over on its side, and pull it through the bait. Then push the eye and the shank deeply into the bait so you feel the hook eye scrape the spine. This hook is now locked into place. Now you have two options. You can let the trailing hook swing freely at this point, but I personally prefer to bury the hook in the meat about an inch above the bait's tail. I bury the trailing hook into the side of the just like I did the top hook. Now you have the herring well protected from tail- and head-biters. When you see how this hook is rigged, with the leader going into the body cavity and out the hole in its side it may appear this rig will easily tear off. This is not the case because the line goes through the short side of the herring, over the back, with the top hook locked into the side of your bait. With your leader going through the short side and over the top of the bait this set-up totally disperses the pressure of a hook tearing out as the current pressure is spread over a large surface area of your bait, including the spine. This roll will give you a slightly larger roll, but it is still a good fish-catching roll.

THE GILLY ROLL: For fast trolling, or for going against heavy current, this is a very durable roll.

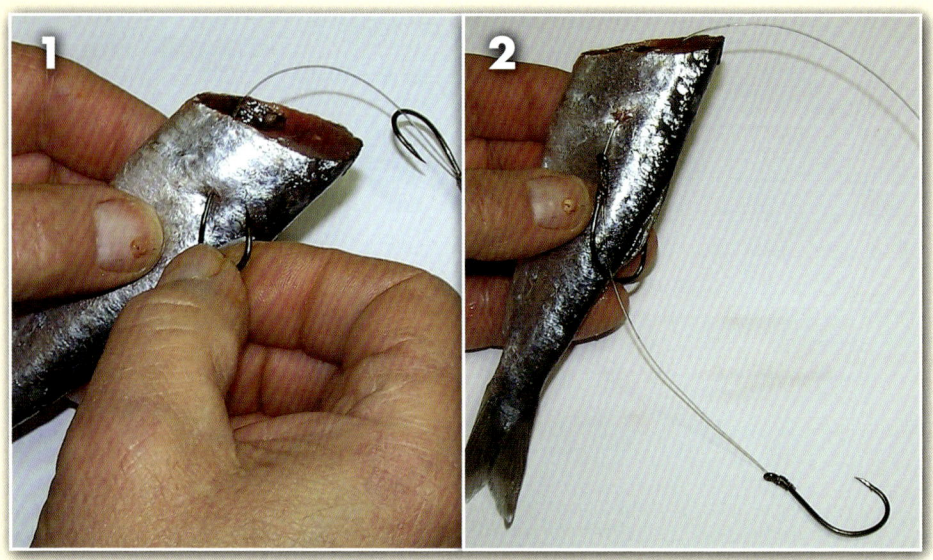

Work the trailing hook deeply into the body cavity on the short side of the bait, and then pull the top hook through the same hole.

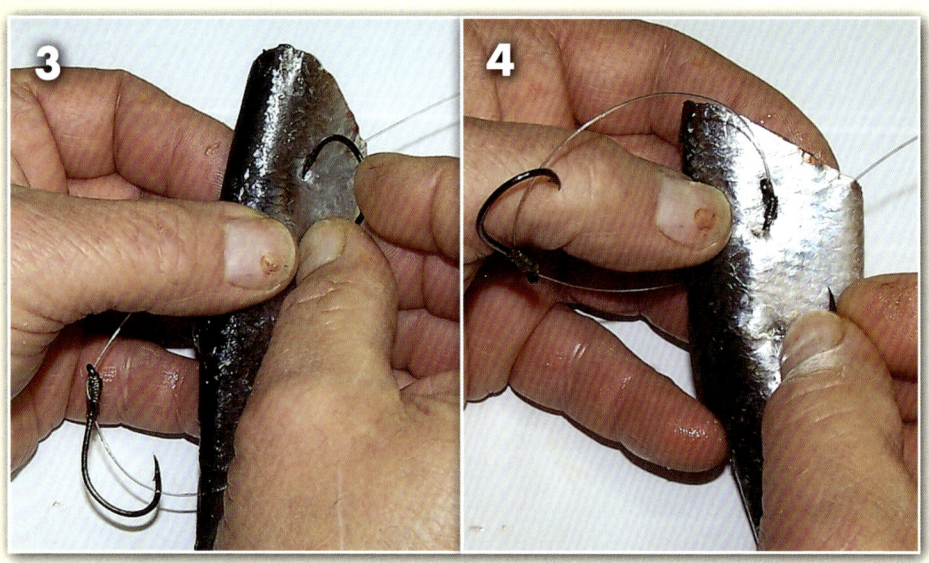

Roll the bait over and work the trailing hook deeply into the bait's side about an inch below the cut, then pull it completely through the bait's side, roll the hook over on its side and pull it through and free of the bait.

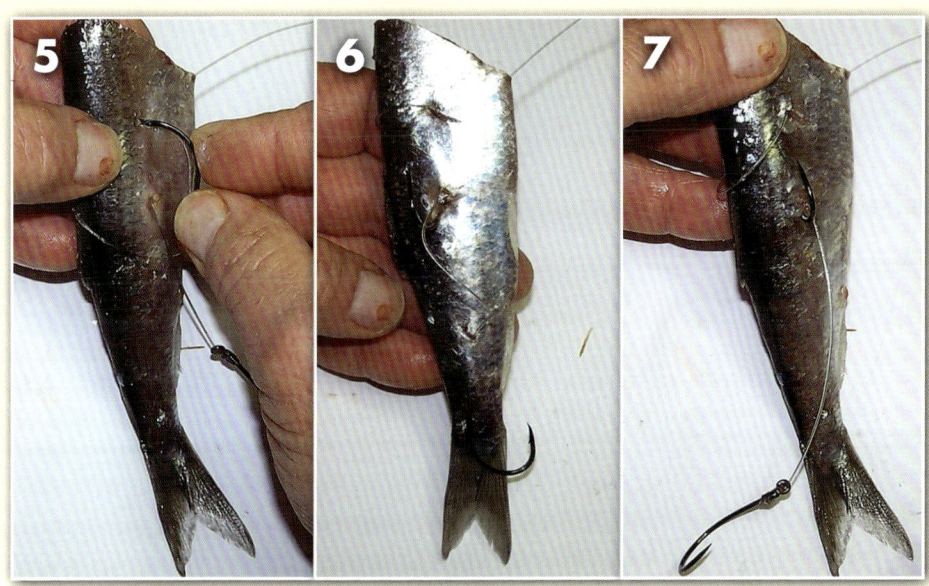

Pull the top hook under the bait's side and push the eye up deeply along the spine until you feel the hook lock into place.

On the Gilly Roll, with the top hook set, you can let the trailing hook dangle freely, or you can bury it about an inch above the tail, or run it through the meat just above the bait's tail and have it hang back slightly longer than the tail.

Since the line goes deeply into the body cavity, over the back and through the bait's opposite side, the tension from high-speed trolling is dissipated over a large area of the bait's spine and flesh. This is a very durable roll.

Rigging A Whole Herring

When rigged correctly you literally cannot tear this bait off your hooks. For many of us, when whole herring are mentioned it conjures up nasty visions of special clips, toothpicks, rubber bands and leaders with sliding top hooks. As Lee Corso likes to say "not so fast, my friend!" Here's a way to rig with the same two hook leaders you normally rig with, and it's so simple and easy to do. Just take your whole herring and pass the trailing hook through the top of the baits eye socket from left to right, and then carefully work the top hook through the eye socket the same way. I try not to knock the eyeballs out of the eye socket, but if they do it's really no big deal. Now I have both hooks hanging freely from the right side of the bait. Depending on the space between the trailing hook and the top hook will dictate where I bury the trailing hook into my bait. Ultimately the top hook will be passed back out through the eye socket after the trailing hook is placed into the bait's flesh, then run through the snout of the bait dead center from top to bottom. So with this in mind it's important to estimate an approximate position of where on the side of your bait to bury the trailing hook, so you have a very slight bend in your bait, and not a severe bend. Once you think you've determined the spot, face the trailing-hook point towards the bait's tail and bury it deeply into the baits flesh at the lateral line. Work the hook point through the flesh, roll the hook over on its side and carefully pull the hook through the bait's flesh. Push the hook eye forward and deeply into the bait's flesh, so you feel the hook eye scrape along the bait's spine, until it pops into place. Then carefully work the top hook back out the eye socket and run the hook through

WHOLE HERRING ROLL: For trolling in the heaviest of currents

Carefully work trailing hook through top of eye socket.

the bait's head, right between the bait's eyes, in a downward motion. Carefully work the barb completely through the bait's jaws, make sure you go through both the upper and lower jaws. By doing this you will keep the bait's lower jaw closed while trolling. With both hooks placed take a look at the bend in your bait. You don't need much of a bend to get your bait to roll, but if the roll is too slow you may need to reposition the trailing hook a little closer to the tail to increase the bend in your bait. If the bend is too severe you may need to move the trailing hook closer to the bait's head. It may take a bait or two to get the spacing and bend perfect, but once you do the roll is bullet proof, and will hold up in the heaviest current or the fastest troll speeds. Once rigged I then inject my whole herring with scent. In past years I've always used Pro-Cure bait oils in herring, anchovy or sardine, but in the last two years I've been using our new Bloody Tuna Oil. Now I'm using Pro-Cure's newest weapon, Water Soluble Fish Oils. The new scents put out a much heavier scent trail in the water, plus they are loaded with amino acids and UV flash. It's an upgrade from the standard fish oils, and once a fish oil is converted to a water-soluble solution, it is much easier for a fish's olfactory receptors to pick up and lock onto than traditional fish oils. But back to injecting a whole herring. I just insert a bait-injector needle up the fish's anal opening and squeeze until the bait's belly swells up. Then I poke three or four holes into the bait's belly, and finally put the injector needle under the bait's gill plate and fill up the bait's head with scent too. This will allow a huge amount of scent to leak out of your bait when trolled.

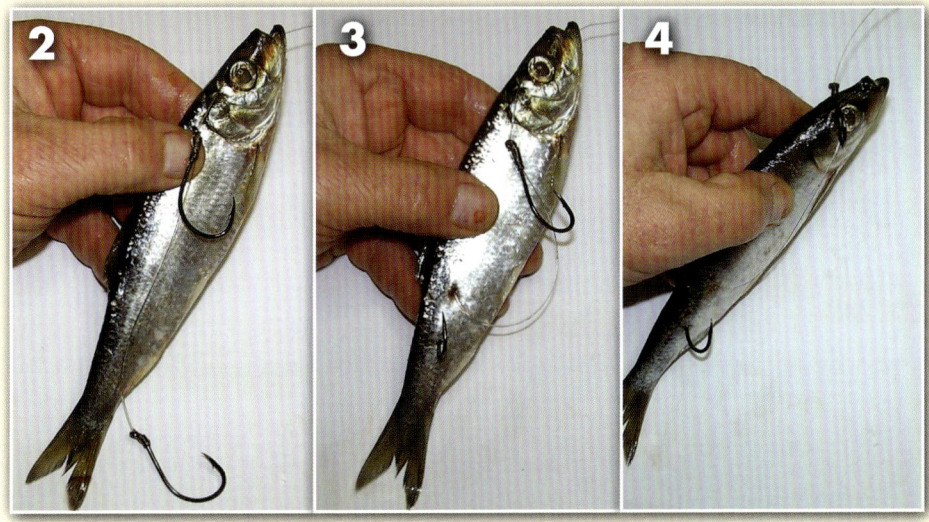

Carefully work top hook through top of eye socket. Bury trailing hook through tall side of bait. Where you set this trailing hook will determine the amount of roll and roll speed you will get when you set the top hook.

Pass top hook back through eye socket and starting right between the bait's eyes work hook point down through head and jaws.

With top hook through bait's jaws, jaws will not open while trolling. The bait shown on the right is a perfect, fast roll. For a slower roll, position the trailing hook closer to the bait's head. With the top hook completely through the bait's head this will handle the heaviest of currents and the fastest troll speed.

HEADHUNTER OR WINGS ROLL

When fishing jetty mouths and ocean bubble areas in late August through October many of our fall Chinook are head hunters. This means they predominantly take their baitfish by the head rather than nipping at or taking it by the tail. Although this method of rigging a herring appears to be quite unorthodox it can be immensely successful, and with a very high hook-up percentage. The first time I saw one of my guide buddies do this I thought he had lost it, but the roll was super tight, and did it get bit. That day we were 7 for 8 on hook-ups. Also the Wings Roll holds up very well in moderate to heavy current, which is another advantage to rigging this way. If you prefer, rather than having both hooks opposite each other near the top of the bait, the placement can be staggered to have one hook near the top and the other hook more towards the tail, just in case you suspect a tail biter or two are out there. When properly rigged, this roll gives a very fast, tight roll. If you prefer to trim the tail fins off your bait the roll is even faster.

HEADHUNTER OR WINGS ROLL

Approximate hook spacing for Wings Roll.

Run trailing hook through spine and out short side of herring.

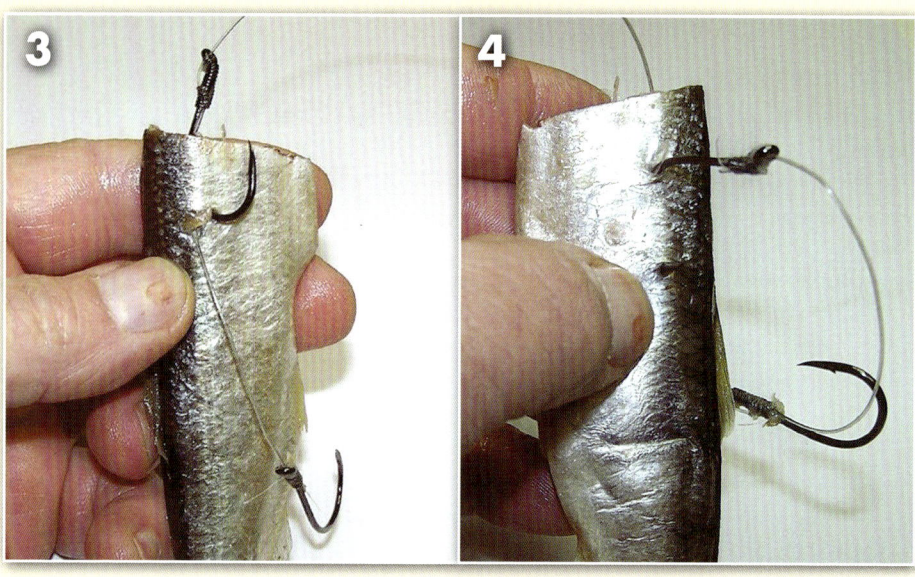

Run top hook through the same hole and out the short side of herring.

Roll the bait over and bury the point of the trailing hook deeply into the side of the herring. As you carefully work the hook through the bait you should feel the hook point scrape on the spine a bit. Pull the hook completely through the bait's side.

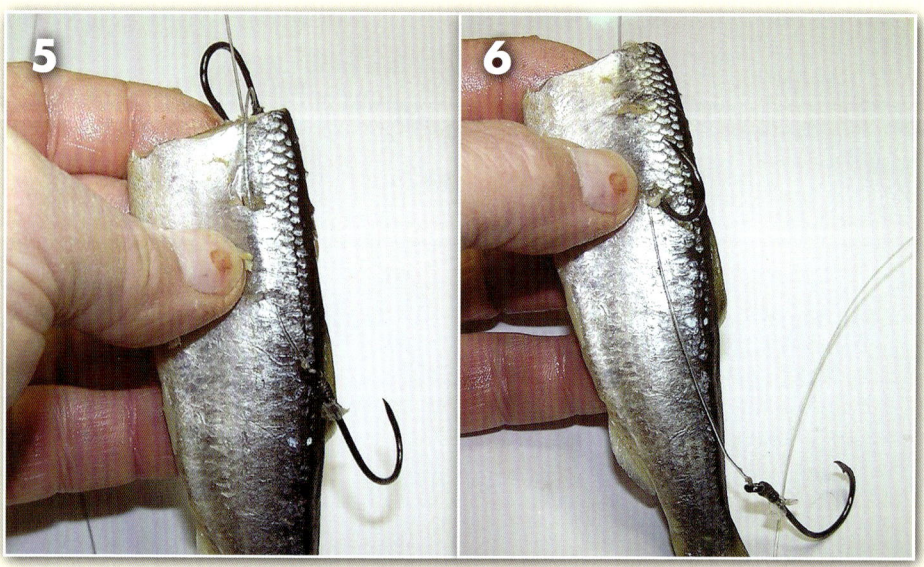

Trailing hook pulled through and free of tall side.

Now bury the top hook into the tall side of the bait, making sure you go through the exact same hole as the first hook.

Bury the trailing hook through the same hole on the short side, and carefully work it through the bait so only the hook point and bend is exposed. With your thumb keeping pressure on top of the bait over where the hook shank is buried, push the hook eye forward to lock it in place.

The short side hook is "locked" into place.

A top view with both wings hooks buried and locked in place.

You can offset the trailing hook more towards the tail if you are concerned about missing tail biters. Just leave a little bit more spacing between your hooks when you are tying your leader.

Different cut angles will give you different rolls. A more angled cut (left) will roll faster, but even the flat cut (right) is a good tight roll.

Adjusting a Roll

Say you want a slightly faster roll so you just speed up your troll speed. BUT what happens when you're trolling in heavy boat traffic and you literally can't speed up. You then need to hand-cut both angles a little more steeply. This will give you a faster roll. If you marry this cut with a top-hook placement very close to the 12 o'clock position on the spine you will get a very fast, tight roll. You can also do the opposite and flatten your cut to get a slower roll, and move your top hook down closer to the 2 or 3 o'clock position. Many times towards the end of the day, or if we've been blessed with limiting out early, and I have leftover baits I will spend a little time on test rolls and different hook placements. Rather than shaking a half dozen leftover herring into the drink as crab bait, I'll try different hand-cut angles and different hook placements. It's a great way to perfect your plug-cut techniques.